BODY

SO

FLURESENT

BODY

SO

FLURESCENT

**AMANDA
CORDNER**

**DAVID
DI GIOVANNI**

PLAYWRIGHTS CANADA PRESS
TORONTO

Body So Fluorescent © Copyright 2023 by Amanda Cordner and David di Giovanni
First edition: March 2023
Printed and bound in Canada by Rapido Books, Montreal

Jacket design by Michel Vrana
Author photo of Amanda Cordner © Dahlia Katz
Author photo of David di Giovanni © Cassandra Rudolph

Playwrights Canada Press
202-269 Richmond St. W., Toronto, ON M5V 1X1
416.703.0013 | info@playwrightscanada.com | www.playwrightscanada.com

LIBRARY AND ARCHIVES CANADA CATALOGUING IN PUBLICATION
Title: Body so fluorescent / Amanda Cordner and David di Giovanni.
Names: Cordner, Amanda, author. | di Giovanni, David, author.
Description: A play.
Identifiers: Canadiana (print) 20230167780 | Canadiana (ebook) 20230167810
  | ISBN 9780369104281 (softcover) | ISBN 9780369104298 (PDF)
  | ISBN 9780369104304 (EPUB)
Classification: LCC PS8605.O734 B63 2023 | DDC C812/.6—dc23

Playwrights Canada Press operates on land which is the ancestral home of the Anishinaabe Nations (Ojibwe / Chippewa, Odawa, Potawatomi, Algonquin, Saulteaux, Nipissing, and Mississauga), the Wendat, and the members of the Haudenosaunee Confederacy (Mohawk, Oneida, Onondaga, Cayuga, Seneca, and Tuscarora), as well as Metis and Inuit peoples. It always was and always will be Indigenous land.

We acknowledge the financial support of the Canada Council for the Arts, the Ontario Arts Council (OAC), Ontario Creates, and the Government of Canada for our publishing activities.

Canada Council   Conseil des arts
for the Arts   du Canada

ONTARIO ARTS COUNCIL
CONSEIL DES ARTS DE L'ONTARIO
an Ontario government agency
un organisme du gouvernement de l'Ontario

Canadä

ONTARIO | ONTARIO
CREATES | CRÉATIF

To Amanda, from David
To David, from Amanda

PLAYWRIGHTS' NOTES

Writing together is as easy as breathing. Our creation process is smooth, deranged, and transformative. We would be hanging out anyway so why not hang out and create art.

We spend so much time talking that the words eventually spill onto the page, creating our stories. Then we turn around and are like, "Oh baby, there it is, we made that. Woah. What were we thinking?"

Body So Fluorescent is the fruit of an old friendship: one that began in a high school drama class between two outsiders. When it came to pick a post-secondary path, we parted ways: one in Toronto, one in Montreal. After eight years, we were reunited. When we finally reconnected, we looked at each other, gave a knowing nod, and began to play.

The power behind this piece comes from the shared fusing of two minds, two energies, two experiences. We believe it's a play where multiple truths can coexist.

We are incredibly grateful for all who have supported this project from its twenty-five minute premiere at the Rhubarb Festival, to its national tour, to its short film iteration, to its publishing. We feel so unbelievably lucky to have our first collaboration bloom into a life of its own.

Amanda Cordner and David di Giovanni

PRODUCTION HISTORY

Body So Fluorescent was first produced as part of the IGNITE! Festival at the Joyce Doolittle Theatre, Calgary, from June 6 to 10, 2017, with the following cast and creative team:

Cast: Amanda Cordner, Felicia Bonée (Jesse Beilman)
Director: David di Giovanni

CHARACTERS

Desiree
Gary
Mess
Shenice

PREFACE

A drag number.

PART ONE

MESS enters. They are dressed in yesterday's party clothes. They search for a specific spot on the stage and find it. They notice the audience. MESS *looks away. They have been caught.*

MESS: I'm just looking for the trigger. The trigger— The moment when— I'm sorry. I'm sorry. I just . . .

> *MESS takes a few breaths, shaking, finding the courage to look up and address the audience.*

(uncontrollably) I was just HERE LAST NIGHT. At the party. I don't wanna interrupt.

(gaining control) But—heh—I must look so bad. I was just here last night at the party, and, heh—don't remember much, but know that I lost my best friend, and know that I feel like shit, and didn't even get laid. And something happened, and I remember her storming off, but I mean, don't really know what . . . the trigger was. And I wasn't . . . myself last night. I never really am, I—become—Shenice.

(slowly transforming) Shenice.

SHENICE emerges.

SHENICE: Shhh-e-neeesssseee. I know, girl. I know. When I'm out, my body becomes hot, hot I'm burning. I am Shenice. Shenice stands like this. Shenice looks at you like *THIS. I AIN'T NO BASIC BITCH.*

Snaps back into MESS.

MESS: I'm sorry. You don't need . . . I don't need . . . Lynn, my therapist, says that vulnerability is power. And I think I need to work on being myself, expressing my true self, not put on masks. And . . . Shenice . . . Shhennicee . . . I just, don't want to, don't need to go there tonight or else I might . . . forget what I do, and, regret what I do, and wind up in yesterday's clothes in front of a group of strangers, trying to retrace my steps. I'm the worst.

Cuz—when I am Shenice, I'm like beaming, my teeth are beaming, I'm confident, sexy, I'm having a good time. People surround me when I'm dancing, and they like, they fucking worship me. They all gather round me, I'm in the middle, popping and grinding, like almost even transcendent. And they're just fighting to get close to me. I've seen deadly fights happen between people who wanted to dance next to me. Someone wound up in a coma. Actually. People literally will kill one another, just to dance up 'gainst—

SHENICE emerges.

SHENICE: *THIS BIG BOOTY.*

SHENICE makes eye contact with a man in the audience.

BOY, CAN YOU HANDLE THIS
EUGH, CAN YOU HANDLE THIS
FUCK, CAN YOU HANDLE THIS
I DON'T THINK YOU CAN HANDLE THIS

> *Hot and energetic soca begins playing. SHENICE begins a*
> *steamy, raunchy dance for the man. As it gets hotter, she*
> *pulls her Spanx up, accentuating her rear. She also exposes*
> *her chest, pulling her shirt past her shoulders. By the*
> *chorus, SHENICE is on the floor, on all fours, rolling for the*
> *man. The soca song slowly fades into a rap, quite low in the*
> *background.*

That's my jam. That's my song. You know, one thing I never
understaaaand about Black celebrities—like Beyoncé, like
Rihanna, like Nicki, how they can step onstage in front of a sea
of millions of white faces, and have those white faces sing along
to their songs, singin' and chantin' "niggah" back at them. Can
you imagine? A sea of white faces all yelling "niggah" back at
you? Niggah. Niggah. Niggah. And that's success yeah? Not me.
Not my idea of success oh no. These white boys and white girls
wish they can dance like me, and oh they try, but they never
gonna match these hips. I met this man at the club last night,
this beautiful Black man, he's givin' me his eyes, I'm dancing for
him, I'm on the stage on all fours, and I'm movin' for him. He
wants me, I can see. He wants to press up 'gainst this. He wants
to spread these cheeks, smack these cheeks, but I'm not that
easy no. I move away, I move toward him, feel his dick against

my ass. He wants to spread these cheeks, smack these cheeks, tear them apart, and stick it in. I'm dancing for him, he's coming closer to me, I'm dancing, dancing, my body glowin' for him. He's coming closer. Then this basic bitch, this white bitch comes up, and starts dancin' with the man. So, I go up to bitch, push bitch outta the way, I say:

You powdery bitch. You milky bitch. You powder. You sugar. You ain't sugar, you aspartame, bitch. You Splenda. You think you got the junk, child, to match this man. He's an anaconda, and you a fuckin' bichon frisé, bitch. Then pixie stick pushes me. The fucking milk bag pushes me and keeps dancin' with MY MAN. Imma cut you. Imma cut you, and Des comes in and she stops . . .

MESS begins a slow transformation back into themselves.

MESS: Desiree comes, and she stops the fight.

I'm sorry . . . I got a little . . . carried away. That's Shenice, I'm sorry. That's me more fun. But uhh . . . here's the boring me . . . and uhh . . . I don't need to perform to get anyone to like me, right? Vulnerability is power. And uh, I don't want to start a fight with any of you. So yeah, I'm gonna . . . try . . . to just be, me, boring me, cuz that's how I'm gonna . . . figure out . . . why . . .

I got a text last night. From Des. Des is my girl who I came here with last night . . . she stopped the fight, and . . . the text . . . It said:

"We're done."

I tried calling but she didn't pick up. I left a message, and I thought if I came back here, it might become . . . clear or, that she'd be here, or someone from that night . . .

Oh god.

MESS *catches their breath.*

I remember . . . going over to her place. She's got this real beautiful place. Like a really nice loft. Like with black leather couches, and like big windows. She's kind of a big deal. And she's got these like big black-and-white prints of the Toronto skyline in her living room, you know, the ones with the pops of colour, like the little bit of red on the CN Tower. I think they're so pretty.

SHENICE *pops up.*

SHENICE: They ugly girl.

Back to MESS.

MESS: I think they're really pretty. And she was a little, like off and distant that night, but started loosening up when she started, she started mixing us drinks. Hehe—get this. She made us vodka Red Bull and champagne drinks. And we must've had like FOUR before we started putting on our clothes. And, god she was so pretty last night, she had this—it was these skin-tight Aztec-design leggings . . . with these platform boots and a black crop top. Her hair was up, and she had these amazing big diamond studs, with this small gold chain round her neck. And oh my god, this aqua-blue eyeliner and these red Monroe lips. The lipstick colour is called Monroe. I chose it for her. And like the aqua-blue and the red-Monroe looked just SO BEAUTIFUL, like with her skin tone.

As SHENICE.

SHENICE: Bitch didn't look nearly as good as me.

Back to MESS.

MESS: Where was I? Right, she looked great. And I looked good too . . . I was wearing, well this *(referring to their clothes)*, but looked more fresh, like my makeup was more fresh, I wasn't as much of a mess as I am now. She put on my makeup, and I put on my weave, clipped it in, because the last time, I used glue, I glued it in, and it actually fell off when I was dancing because of the sweat. Ew. So yeah, clipped it in, looked in the mirror, and I looked so hot. Des even came behind me and she started clapping for me! She said, WORK IT GIRL. And I was all YOU KNOW, I KNOW GURL, I'M GONNA TWERK HARD TONIGHT. AND JUST YOU WAIT NEXT MONTH WHEN OUR ASSES ARE IN CUBA. And we laughed and kept dancing. The cab came. We got in. We got out. I stepped out of that cab . . . as . . . Shenice.

As SHENICE.

SHENICE: Got my crown on, my girl followin' me, we walked in, we didn't even need no people checkin' us, they made room for us. Had my crown on and walked in . . .

As MESS.

MESS: Through there.

We walked in right through there, I felt like I had my crown on and people made way for us.

SHENICE walks towards the entrance.

No wait, there was music playing so hard too.

Hip hop begins blaring. She struts down the ramp again. When she arrives at the stage, the music stops.

Then . . . right, then she went to get a drink. That's when I saw the man, the handsome Black man. He was right over . . . there. And he came to walk up to me over here. That's when I was dancing and started the . . . the fight . . . with that—basic bitch. And Desiree came up to me here. She took us to the bathroom, we touched up our makeup. Then she started takin' me to the bar, but I . . . said . . .

SHENICE: GIRL THIS BOOTY NEEDS A SLAVE. GET SHENICE A DRINK. I'LL BE ON STAGE.

MESS: Right, I walked up to the stage. People made way for me and I walked straight onto the stage. That's where we like to dance.

SHENICE: BITCH. That's where we live.

Slow and sexy transcendent hip hop begins to play. SHENICE is dancing.

I was GLOWING.

MESS: Geez it was so crowded, and I kept dancing . . . yeah, as Shenice, right. I forget, did I . . . ? Oh my god right, "BOOTYLI-CIOUS" came on, and like shit,

HALF MESS, HALF SHENICE: I started dancing and like everyone was orbiting around me, just trying to dance with me. Right, and then that basic bitch was on stage, and I gave him such a stank face, and kept dancing, and get this, PIXIE STICK tries to take my place centre stage. Doin' these awkward boney twerks. Get the fuck outta the way.

SHENICE: You get everything bitch. You take our men, you take our style, you take our fuckin' dance moves. Make room for the Black woman. MAKE ROOM FOR THIS BLACK WOMAN.

MESS: And out the corner of my eye I saw Des with two drinks in her hand . . . right she, she was at the edge of the stage here. And she had this look on her face . . . like—

MESS *makes the face.*

She had the two drinks in her hand and she goes HERE.

And she just stormed away. I was like, what?? And saw her walking down the floor, over there. I like pushed after her and grabbed her arm. I was like, "Des, what's up"—wait, no, I was all:

SHENICE: "What's wrong girl?" And my sister, my girl, turned to me with so much anger and she say:

DESIREE: Drop the act. I'm not your GURL. Let go of my arm, white boy.

SHENICE: Who you callin' white boy? We togetha with these fuckin' pixie sticks here.

DESIREE: No. Just no. Let me go 'kay? Have a fucking blast to-night. I hope you get fucked. I hope your little white-boy ass gets fucked while you pretend it's Black.

SHENICE: You don't mean that girl. You just havin' a bad day. Time of the month, am I right? I know. I know.

DESIREE: You don't know. It's not funny anymore. You look like a damn fool.

SHENICE: But this me. Shenice's yo main bitch.

DESIREE: Gary. Gary. This isn't you. The real you is a little fag from nowhere Ontario. You are not a woman. You are not Black. You are NOT a Black woman. So don't fucking claim either.

SHENICE: *(with gusto)* BIIIITCH You just jealous that I do it better than you.

>   *DESIREE slaps SHENICE.*

(to the audience) She fuckin' slapped me so hard that my weave fell out.

>   *A piece of SHENICE's hair falls to the ground.*

DESIREE: That's where you're wrong. You can't do IT better, if you don't know what it IS.

MESS: Des, hey, Shenice IS the REAL ME. I am more myself than ever. And, I sort of do understand what it's like to feel Black . . . I mean, I don't but I kind of do. I don't get this. Can we just have fun again?

DESIREE leaves. MESS melts into GARY.

GARY: My name is Gary King. Kids at school called me Fairy King. Haha, so funny. I'm from Inglewood, Ontario, which no offence should be burnt. I miss my mom, but my dad didn't really talk to me. I love The Pussycat Dolls. I moved to Toronto as soon as I could, went to school, and I'm working at a vegan bakery now. I met Des at school, and she . . . I . . . look up to her and don't understand because Des, I look up to her, I'm not making fun, I admire her, I'm not making fun, I want to be like her.

SHENICE: Ladies, what up ladies that's right. We in the ladies room tonight. Ladies' problems, that's right ladies. If you in a relationship, and you know that it won't matter in a day's time, in a week's time, in a year's time, you know what you say, you say, YOU KNOW WHAT? It ain't no thing. It's a hair flip. And you flip your hair and you move on, that's right. It's a hair flip. It's whatever. It's a hair flip. I flip my hair and I move on.

(sucks her teeth) She just a jealous bitch. She just a jealous, whitewashed bitch. She say she Black, but she talk like a white girl, dress like a white girl, fuck like a white girl, dance like a white girl

and she BLACK? Ain't nobody got time for that. Pat that weave, pat that weave, pat that weave. GURL GURL GURL GURL GURLLLL, MHMM MHMM MHMM MHMM.

GARY: I'm sorry.

GARY leaves.

INTERLUDE

A drag queen comes on stage to perform a song.

PART TWO

DESIREE is sitting in her room with her phone in front of her.

DESIREE: I just feel like I'm responsible.

And that I should just listen to the voicemail because he's probably calling for my help. And I just ignored it last night.

I don't know, I just can't pick it up, I can't give him a call.

What's wrong with me?

I was off last night. Why? I made this date. And then I cancelled it, cuz Gary was . . .

He had a bad week. So we booked this trip to Cuba. He tried to . . . I mean he hasn't been in a good place for the last few weeks, and I needed to be there for him, you know, dance with him, be his . . . well . . . fag hag.

It wasn't a big deal, I just rescheduled the date. Just reschedule the date, pay for the trip, and go to a gay bar. That's fine. But that's not why I'm angry at him . . . I . . .

It's . . . about 7 p.m. He arrives. He looks so frail, like if I hug him too hard, he'd just shatter.

He's gotten worse. I mean he's always been, like, a little, delicate. But when I first met him, he lit up like a, I don't know, like a glow stick that was just cracked and turned on. First year of college. And we'd have coffee together, and he'd just keep on glowing, and I started glowing too. And the first night we got drinking, went out dancing, holy shit I've never had that much fun in my life.

He'd go like:

YOU'RE SO FUCKING HAWT. BITCH YES, FUCK JOEY—Joey had just left me—FUCK HIM, YOU'RE A DAMN GODDESS DIVINE. YOU ARE LIKE DESIREE QUEEN OF THE FUCKING GREAT LAKES.

We went to this gay bar . . . holy shit . . .

Bright wet flesh. Colours bouncing off their skin. And beards with lipstick, and pearl necklaces with wife beaters, and hair sculpted like . . . like French gardens. And I walked in that club and the universe stopped.

Everyone's eyes turned, and, the DJ just started a new track, it was . . . RIGHT it was Rihanna. "We found love in a hopeless place." You know the beginning . . .

And the sea of men parted, and they all adored me. And when I started dancing, they made a circle around me, and it was like a fucking dance kingdom, where one man would like vogue with me, AND I WOULD WIN THE VOGUE BATTLE, and he would leave, and another would come, AND I'D WIN AGAIN, I WAS FUCKING DESIREE QUEEN OF THE GREAT LAKES.

Gary would scream that. Cabs would pass us and he would scream:

(as GARY) DO YOU KNOW WHO SHE IS? SHE'S FUCKING DESIREE QUEEN OF THE GREAT LAKES AND PATRON SAINT OF FABULOUS FAGS.

    DESIREE laughs.

Yeah I love him. What's wrong with me then?

Des just pick up the phone, just listen to your friend, just call him back. He's hasn't been in a good place, I was just off last night, fuck we had vodka Red Bull champagne drinks, we were just . . . not in the right place.

Then he takes out this bag . . .

GARY: You've been so good to me Des, so good to me. I just need to dance, and like have a great night, I know that's what I need to do, and things will start pulling themselves together. I need to like just have fun, and you know treat myself. That's what my therapist says. And you'll never guess what I bought with all my tip money.

DESIREE: What?

GARY: The perfect outfit to slay.

DESIREE: Was it bad that my eyes rolled a little? He didn't see. And when he goes out, he like . . . starts to act . . . ghetto? And it's funny, it's always been sorta funny. And when he starts to act like that, you know, he's usually wearing like, maybe a piece of jewellery or like some shit in his hair, or some like wild makeup. But when he got out of the bathroom . . .

SHENICE struts out.

GARY/SHENICE: So what do you think?

DESIREE: I'm awful. I said, "Werk it gurl."

SHENICE: Bitch right, Shenice gonna destroy some bitches tonight.

DESIREE: I was sick to my stomach. He looked like a slutty clown. And he looked in the mirror, and he sucked his teeth like:

DESIREE imitates it.

I thought . . .

Is he modelling himself off some idea he has of who I am?

She sucks her teeth.

I have never sucked my teeth IN MY LIFE. And I honestly thought, is this kid more Black than me?

She sucks her teeth.

Did I want to be Black like him? Which is crazy cuz he's not. He's not, I am, but . . . woah this is complicated.

At that moment, through the mirror, I made eyes with him. But it wasn't him. It was . . . something else . . . like possessed. And I just looked away.

SHENICE: Yo gurl, wha gwan wha gwan?

DESIREE: I said, "Just a little tired."

SHENICE: Imma make you move tonight. Imma teach you how to slay.

DESIREE: Right, fag teach me how to slay.

    DESIREE covers her mouth.

I'm sorry. I didn't actually say that. I mean, maybe I thought it. I was in a bad mood. And he looked like a fool. Which means that Des, DES QUEEN OF THE GREAT LAKES AND PATRON SAINT OF FABULOUS FAGS has to be fucking SECURITY GUARD OF UNSTABLE FRIENDS.

You don't get it, he was casting me in that role. Even when the cab came. The driver was looking at Gary through the mirror. I made eyes with the driver, eyes that said:

DUDE YOU BETTER KEEP DOSE EYES ON THE ROAD.

You know, if Gary and me were like characters in a TV show,

he'd be the main character, that's just how it is. He used to call us Thelma and Louise, but in truth I'm just the fucking car.

I turned to look at Gary. He was just looking out the window. He saw that I was looking at him, he turned to look at me . . . and reached out to touch my hand.

I looked toward the window. Des pull yourself together, just go out tonight, have fun. Tonight, have fun.

We got to the party. It was called Birds of Paradise. Of course. Gary, or, you know, SHENICE vaults out of the cab, and get this, there's a line of people in the rain to get into this party, and he moves right up to the bouncer, I'm behind, holding our coats, the bouncer lets us in!

Music is blaring. It's Taylor Swift. Oh god. Shenice turns to me and says:

"I don't mean no disrespect, but Beyoncé had the best music video of all time."

That's funny. It's so funny. And when he gets like this, holy shit, I laugh until I snort. Oh my god, the first time he like, started . . . I guess talking to me like he was a Black girl . . . it was like he was saying things I've thought my WHOLE LIFE.

SHENICE: *(referring to the audience)* These white boys just jealous of us.

DESIREE: *(laughing)* That's exactly how I felt.

SHENICE: *(referring to the audience)* These pixie sticks dance like a fucking Protestant pastor having an orgasm.

DESIREE: Yes yes yes, they do, they fucking do.

SHENICE: There's three kinds of white boys. The straight ones dance like they a wooden fence on a windy day. The gay ones dance like they're in a fucking Chanel commercial, and everyone else dance like Backstreet comin' back, but they ain't EVER COMIN' BACK.

Nah nah, me n you gurl, we make dese bitches bow down.

DESIREE: *(to the audience)* RIGHT GURL,

"BOW DOWN BITCHES
BOW BOW DOWN BITCHES
BOW DOWN BITCHES
BOW BOW DOWN BITCHES"

Oh. Shit. Uhh . . . what are you even looking at?

Oh my god, right, this is so fucked up:

We walk into the club . . . the lights are spastic, light dark light dark, and when it's light, it's just, I just see white, almost dismembered body parts, sometimes grabbing, stretching, gyrating, and then it goes dark, and back light again. When it's light, I see their makeup, dark around their eyes, screaming the songs with their teeth, biting the music, and it goes dark. The DJ is dressed like a bird . . . wearing these enormous . . . like wings, and they're pink and green, and he has a dildo on his head, like a strap-on that he's put around his temples, and the dildo just falls down past his nose.

I step in the room, and nobody notices.

Nicki Minaj comes on. The lights go dark, they go back on, and suddenly all of the bodies are black, they're black body parts, and this "Shenice" is already halfway to the stage, where she's gonna fucking own the dance floor. I follow.

I try to dance, I'm so out of it. Some hand grabs my ass. I dance away. Some bitch falls on me, I put him back on his feet. A boy comes yelling in my ear, what's he saying:

"YOU'RE FIERCE."

I haven't done anything yet to be fierce. But okay. I'm fierce.

I move away, I try to find Gary . . .

Over there. Shit I was playing his fucking security guard all night. Bitch was starting fights with this other small twinky boy. They could have been brothers. That's right, he told me to get him a drink. And I did. I always do. I bought him . . . like five drinks that night. I had two drinks in my hand, and he was yelling at this twink . . .

Right there. I sneak through black arms and legs, eyes and hair. The song changes. It's Bieber, and holy shit, the lights go dark, and flash up, the bodies, the arms the legs, the hips, they're as white as ghosts. Where the fuck am I? Some finger touches my ass. I move away. Some bitch falls on me, I put him back to his feet. Someone comes to yell in my ear, what does he say:

"Can I touch your hair?"

I move toward Shenice, she's in this fight with . . . this white boy, oh my god. I grab Shenice, right around her chest, and move her away.

SHENICE: Bitch wants to take my man, shit.

DESIREE: And I say to her, Shenice, let's get the fuck out of here.

Why was I talking to her like she was Shenice? It was like, we were the only two Black women in the club.

Let's fucking split.

SHENICE: Nah gurl, that pixie stick wants to take my man, nobody take Shenice's man.

DESIREE: Okay fine. But no more fights. Just chill.

SHENICE: I'm chill, I'm chill.

DESIREE: Right. I go to get us some drinks. Shenice is following behind, until, right it's Beyoncé. "Drunk in Love." The beginning of it, the crowd goes wild, flapping their arms around. Someone rubs my ass to the music like . . .

DESIREE imitates it.

At this moment, the lights go out, and they come back on, I don't even know what colour their skin is. It's just a dense mass, colourless, formless, it's a bad feeling, it's sick to my stomach.

I somehow make it to the bar . . . push some bodies out of the way . . . somehow blurt out TWO VODKA SODAS. The body behind the bar says something that sounds like:

"Aisha gets what Aisha wants."

I think I say fuck off, and somehow have the drinks in my hand, I don't know forward from backward.

MOVE OUTTA MA WAY BITCH, LET THE BLACK WOMAN THROUGH THIS FUCKIN' MESS. TIGHTY WHITIES MOVE!

Did I really say that? "Tighty whities move?" What does that even mean?

I move toward the door.

"HUNNIE where do you think you're going with those drinks?"

I turn toward the bouncer. I scoff at him. I put the drinks on the floor. He gives me this totally extra look like:

DESIREE imitates it.

I go outside to get some fresh air. It's still raining outside, but I

walk out of the bar, I stand under like an awning of some con-
venience store. The streetlights are blaring like flashlights. Drunk
boys and girls walk up and down the strip.

I feel . . . so fucking lonely. And forgotten. Because, you know, HE'S
NOT A BLACK WOMAN. HE GETS TO PLAY PRETEND AND PUT ON
SLUTTY OUTFITS, BUT THE TRUTH IS, HE GETS TO PLAY PRETEND
WHEN HE WANTS TO, AND I DON'T GET TO PRETEND I'M BLACK AND
I DON'T GET TO PRETEND I'm a WOMAN. I'm a Black woman always.
I'm reminded that I'm Black every time I'm on any dance floor. I'm
reminded that I'm a woman when he jiggles my titties, but it's okay
because he's GAY. AND I'm especially reminded I'm a Black woman,
when, in a room full of beautiful men, I get played with like a toy
on the dance floor, and then I'm left completely alone at the end of
it, at 1 a.m. in the morning, when they're all hooking up with one
another. And I was used. In some kind of . . . mating ritual.

My phone lights up, a text . . . from Gary. OH MY GOD RIGHT! For
a split second, I think, do I even know a Gary? I remember getting
the text . . . I looked down, and it said:

"Where you at niggah?"

Before I can even like think to really read it, I am writing, "coming in." And that's when it hits me. Gary. Gary King. Gary the frail
kid I sat beside in school, Gary the boy I took out for a manicure
the first time he had sex, Gary the boy who showed up breakable
at my apartment just a few hours ago, Gary the gay kid from
Inglewood, Ontario, just called me niggah.

And I replied. With servitude.

Sailing through this world is hard. There are things you don't know are offensive or why they're offensive until, like sticky vodka soda under your shoes, it just keeps pch pch pch, and you begin to wonder, why am I feeling like this?

> *She goes into the audience, and facing the empty stage she asks:*

"Where you at niggah"
"Where you at niggah"
"Where you at niggah"

I go back into the bar. The two drinks have been kicked over. Right, "Bootylicious" is playing. I go to the bar, pay for two more. I see Gary just so blissful in the centre of the stage, a smile that's uncomplicated.

And I want to be where he is. I want to be in the middle of the stage, dancing without one fucking care. I want to dress like a fool, and I want to be Shenice, I want to not give a fucking damn and suck my teeth at whoever the fuck I want, and push bitches out of the way, and be so unforgiving.

So I go, I push past the crowd, I'm headed for the stage, I'm at the very edge, and like bright molten lava spills out of me:

"YOU TAKE EVERYTHING BITCH. YOU TAKE OUR MEN. YOU TAKE OUR STYLE. YOU TAKE OUR FUCKING DANCE MOVES. MAKE ROOM FOR THE BLACK WOMAN. MAKE ROOM FOR THIS BLACK WOMAN."

Or was that Shenice?

And I whipped my drink at him.

>*She imitates it.*

Ice and all. I just fucking whipped it at him—like this. *(imitates it)* And oh my god, that's right! SHENICE . . . SHENIIIIIIIIIICEEE . . . went from:

>*DESIREE puts on SHENICE.*

And when I whipped my drink at him.

>*Slow motion we see SHENICE melt into GARY.*

And we fought. I just remember saying:

"You're not Black. You're not Black. Bitch, you're not Black."

I slapped him.

We were right outside the club, what did he even say, I can't even really remember. Something like, you're jealous.

What am I jealous of?

And that's when I slapped him, and it felt good. Too good. I could have fucking ripped his weave out, brought his face against the wet concrete, and just rub his skin against the sidewalk . . . I could have just scrubbed his makeup off with the sidewalk, and grate past his imaginary skin tone—

I'm sorry, okay.

And I left. I went home. He tried calling a few times. I saw that he left a voicemail. I woke up this morning, and I can't check it. I can't check it.

You know, he probably hooked up with that Black guy last night. He probably spent the night getting fucked, and was just calling me to talk about it after . . .

He probably pretends he's Black when he has sex even.

Rolling his hips like this . . .

All like:

SHENICE: OHH JAMAL

WAIT WHAT?

OHH LASHAWN?

WAIT WHAT?

OH JAMAL JAMAL. I LOVE YOU, JAMAL. MMM. BOW DOWN TO THIS ASS.

FUCK, SO HOT LIKE A JUNGLE IN HERE.

SLAP IT, WHIP IT, WORSHIP IT.
SLAP IT, WHIP IT, WORSHIP IT.
SLAP IT, WHIP IT, WORSHIP IT.

> *Back to* DESIREE.

DESIREE: What? Don't look at me like that. I just wouldn't be surprised if he was that insensitive. Calling me to tell me all about it . . .

What?

> *A long beat.*

But what if he's not okay? I mean what if he . . . it's awful, I know it's awful to think . . . but I can't help but feel SO GUILTY, for leaving him alone there . . . what if he tried to . . .

Like if he called me, crying, like passed out in some park, screaming into his phone.

Lying down in some like twisted position,

> DESIREE *lies down.*

And is crying like:

GARY: DEESSSSSSSS
DESSSSSSSSS
DESSS IT'S MEEEEEEE

I'M SORRY WILL YOU JUST PICK UP THE PHONE,

WHY DON'T YOU PICK UP, I'M SORRY OKAY.

GURRL. GURRRRLLLLLLLLLL. YO YO GURRRRLLL. PLEEASEEEEEE.

I FUCKING LOVE YOU. PLEASE. DES JUST PICK UP THE PHONE GURL, C'MON.

I'M NOT OKAY RIGHT NOW. OKAY? I'M NOT OKAY.

SERIOUSLY I WOUND UP, IN SOME, FUCKING, BACK ALLEY. I WAS BEAT UP BY A GROUP OF GUYS, THEY TOOK MY FUCK-ING PURSE, THEY TOOK MY MONEY, THEY TOOK MY FUCKING PHOOOOOOOOOOONNNNNNNNNEEEEEEEE.

DESIREE: I mean, probably not the phone part. Cuz how would he have called me? I'm probably just overexaggerating. And you know, I can't always be his saviour, and I can't build my life around helping him, you know he needs to learn to help himself. I'm always his stage, I'm always the one holding those heels up.

We go out. YAS QUEEN. C'MON GURL LET'S GO TO SOME FAGGY BAR.

   DESIREE slowly becomes Shenice-ish.

GET ME A DRANK GURL. HOLD THIS BITCH'S FURRRRRR. And I do. I hold the coat in the corner while he's on stage grinding with dudes, looking to pick up. He's up there soo happy. Sooo happy.

But I ain't nobody's niggah. When DESIREE dance, she dance for nobody but Desiree. When Desiree talk, she don't need to please you. When Desiree arrives, there ain't no room for feelin' sad fo yourself, Desiree is here, Desiree don't feel sad, she don't feel worthless, she don't feel helpless. Desiree can pick up the phone. Desiree afraid of no voicemail, Desiree just press DELETE, after rollin' her eyes havin' to take two minutes out of her life to listen to otha people. Desiree picks up her phone . . .

Desiree ain't afraid, she ain't sad, and Desiree ain't guilty. Desiree don't feel like she responsible fo otha fools actin' like fools. Desiree don't think:

"Maybe I should have said something earlier."

NO. That kinda thinkin' is for haters. What? Imma listen, I don't care, Imma listen . . .

White bitch askin' me to press one, Imma do it.

> *She listens. In listening,* DESIREE *melts back into herself.*
>
> *A long beat.* DESIREE *looks at her phone.*
>
> *Lights begin to fade.*

GARY: *(whispering and high)* Desss. Desss. Hey it's me. I was just thinking about our trip, and how excited I am for it. Cuba's gonna be so fun, and warm, and like we're totally gonna be the best fucking dancers on the resort, right? Right?

I just have this gut feeling that you're gonna find someone there. I know, I know I always say that, but like, I just have this feeling that you're gonna find someone there. We're gonna have so much sex. And like, see the ocean. God so excited for the ocean. Des, I'm gonna like baptize you in the ocean, Des queen of the Atlantic. And from there, we have to go to the West Coast. If I ever make enough money, we'll go to the Indian Ocean too . . . the Arctic after. And oh em gee, you'll be Des EMPRESS of ALL OCEANS, and PATRON SAINT . . . PATRON SAINT of . . . people stuck in dark places, PATRON SAINT of gays who are falling into graves. Sorry . . . sorry I don't mean to get so dark . . . I don't mean it that way, you just mean a lot to me. We're like Thelma and Louise.

(yawns) Oh my god it's been such a long week. I'm like . . . I don't even know where I am, I'm on some street, I probably look like a mess. I'm actually sitting on a curb with puddles next to me . . . I can't even see myself in them. I want to check myself but the sun is sparkling in my eyes so I can't see how messed I must look. I wouldn't be surprised if I just got sunburned sitting here . . . well . . . I'll be ready for Cuba!

(yawning) I'm so tired . . . Will you call me back tomorrow? Goodbye. Bye. Goodbye. Bye. Bye.

EPILOGUE

After the curtain call, ACTOR comes on stage.

ACTOR: If you have two minutes, I'd like to tell you what happens to Gary and Des. They meet up. They had made plans to meet the following week . . . yes Des called Gary back—but someone postponed, and then the other did, and they finally met up the next month. Gary suggested trying the holiday lattes at the Starbucks around the corner from his work. Des was early, so she popped into Gary's work. Gary had his hair coloured, that's the first thing they spoke about. When he got off work, they went down the street. There was lots of silence, awkward smiling, in the line. They ordered a drink, Gary insisted on paying. When they sat down, he finally apologized.

"Do you know what you're apologizing for?"
"Is it Shenice?"
"Yah."
"I'm sorry about Shenice. I won't do that anymore."
"Thanks."

They fell out of touch the following year . . . you know, happy birthdays, thinking of you's. They did go to Cuba together. Shenice came out twice, Des didn't say anything. Des got a promotion, moved to Vancouver, and Gary . . . we actually don't know what happened to him. He was talking to his mom on the phone one night. He hung up. She forgot that she wanted to ask him something, called him back fifteen minutes later, and he didn't pick up. He just disappeared into thin air.

ACKNOWLEDGEMENTS

First and foremost, this play would not have been created without the support and guidance of Mel Hague. Thank you for taking a chance on the seed of an idea, and for supporting its growth and development. Thank you also to Charles Netto and the folks at the IGNITE! Festival in Calgary, who were the first to take a chance on programming the full sixty-minute version. Each opportunity to perform the play strengthened it, so a big thank you to all of the folks who hosted us across the country: Laura Nanni, Eda Holmes, Guy de Carteret, Thea James, Dave Mott, and a few others. An enormous THANK YOU goes to Catherine Hernandez and b current for being the first company to commit to programming this play in a theatre season. Catherine was also instrumental in supporting the ongoing development of the play throughout the pandemic. Thanks to Sadie Berlin, Marcel Stewart, and daniel carter for keeping the dream of a Buddies premiere alive. Thanks to Barry, Angie, Ettorino, and Silvana for all the love and support; Simon for your love, design, and patience; and Bilal for being an advocate for this story.

Amanda Cordner is a Toronto-based creator and performer. Within her company Madonnanera, Amanda and creative partner David di Giovanni developed and toured the award-winning solo show *Body So Fluorescent* across North America. Madonnanera's second show, *Wring the Roses*, was featured in Why Not Theatre's RISER Project in 2019. Amanda is also pursuing a career in film and television as a creator and actor. Her company adapted *Body So Fluorescent* into a short film in 2020, which was presented at the Inside Out Film Festival and won the Emerging Canadian Artist Award. TV credits include *Sort Of*, *The Expanse*, and *Baroness von Sketch Show*.

David di Giovanni is a theatre director and creator currently living in Toronto. He holds an MFA in Theatre Directing from York University. In 2017, he co-founded Madonnanera, a rich creative collaboration with Amanda Cordner that is invested in making outrageous and intersectional theatre work. He has won awards for Outstanding Direction, Outstanding Play, and Outstanding Production (*NOW Magazine*'s Best of SummerWorks) and Emerging Canadian Artist (Inside Out) for *Body So Fluorescent* and was nominated for Outstanding Ensemble (Dora Mavor Moore Awards) for *Wring the Roses*.